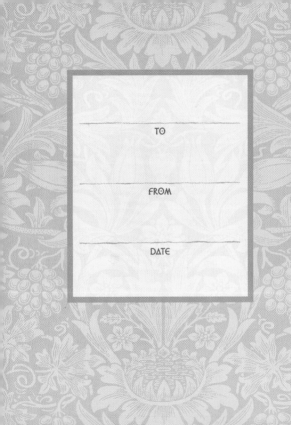

TO

FROM

DATE

LITTLE ONES
COLLECTION

LITTLE PROMISES FROM ABOVE

Photography © 1998 by Virginia Dixon

Text copyright © 1998 by Garborg's, Inc.

Design by Thurber Creative

Published by Garborg's, Inc.
P. O. Box 20132, Bloomington, MN 55420

ISBN 1-881830-756

Printed in Hong Kong

Little Promises
from Above

There are moments when our hearts
nearly burst within us for the sheer
joy of being alive.... Moments like
these renew in us a heartfelt
appreciation for life.

GWEN WEISING

May you grow to be as beautiful
as God meant you to be when
He first thought of you.

I am beginning to learn that it is the
sweet, simple things of life which
are the real ones after all.

LAURA INGALLS WILDER

Be on the lookout for mercies....
Blessings brighten when we
count them.

MALTBIE D. BABCOCK

Love,
consolation,
and peace
bloom only
in the garden
of sweet
contentment.

MARTHA
ANDERSON

"For I know the plans I have for you,"
declares the Lord, "plans to prosper
you and not to harm you,
plans to give you hope and a future."

JEREMIAH 29:11 NIV

Only God can keep all His promises.

JANETTE OKE

Where your pleasure is, there is
your treasure; where you treasure,
there your heart; where your heart,
there your happiness.

AUGUSTINE

Every person's life is a fairy tale
written by God's fingers.

HANS CHRISTIAN ANDERSEN

*Joy is
the serious
business
of heaven.*

C. S. LEWIS

We are ever so secure
in God's everlasting arms.

When you have...
accomplished your daily
task, go to sleep in peace.
God is awake.

VICTOR HUGO

God's promises
are like the stars;
the darker the night
the brighter they shine.

DAVID NICHOLAS

We are all precious
in His sight.

Each dawn holds a new hope
for a new plan, making the start of
each day the start of a new life.

GINA BLAIR

May the God of hope fill you with all
joy and peace as you trust in him.

ROMANS 15:13 NIV

Lift up your eyes.
Your heavenly Father waits
to bless you—in inconceivable ways
to make your life what you never
dreamed it could be.

ANNE ORTLUND

Love is the reason behind
everything God does.

God puts each fresh morning, each
new chance of life, into our hands as
a gift to see what we will do with it.

Great is his faithfulness;
his lovingkindness begins
afresh each day.

LAMENTATIONS 3:23 TLB

Always new. Always exciting.
Always full of promise. The
mornings of our lives, each a
personal daily miracle!

GLORIA GAITHER

Every moment is full of wonder,
and God is always present.

God has promised strength for the day,
Rest for the labor, light for the way,
Grace for the trials, help from above,
Unfailing sympathy, undying love.

ANNIE JOHNSON FLINT

All things work together for good
to those who love God.

ROMANS 8:28 NKJV

There is no
safer place
to be than in
the Father's
hands.

Where there is faith,
there is love.
Where there is love,
there is peace.
Where there is peace,
there is God.
Where there is God,
there is no need.